The Bristol
Treasure Island Trail

Long John Silver Trust

Layout design by William Fairney and Sally Mundy

First Edition 2005
Second edition published in 2008 by
Black Spot Publishing, an Imprint of Diesel Publishing
The Long John Silver Trust
C/o The Beaufort Arms
High Street
Hawkesbury Upton
South Glos.
GL9 1AU

ISBN 978-0-9554455-3-8

Printed and Bound by Cpod, Trowbridge, Wiltshire BA14 0XB, UK

www.longjohnsilvertrust.co.uk

This book is dedicated
to the memory of
Frank Shipsides esq. M.A.
1908 - 2005

The Pirate King
— Almost —

The Bristol Treasure Island Trail

This book has been produced by The Long John Silver Trust,
co-founded by Mark Steeds (Secretary) and Gerry Brooke (Chairman)
Written and researched by Mark Steeds, Gerry Brooke and Bill Fairney
Photographs from the Long John Silver Trust collection
Illustrations of ships by Dru Marland
Cover and Bristol Treasure Island Trail Map by Adrian Blenkiron
Second edition Edited by Bill Fairney

As part of the Great Reading Adventure, organised by Bristol City Council in 2003, free, abridged copies of Treasure Island were distributed to every school in the city.

An enjoyable time was had by all when Hawkesbury Primary School in South Gloucestershire kindly allowed Herbie Rawlings and Mark Steeds, from the Long John Silver Trust, to read Stevenson's exciting novel to the whole school. By re-instating dialogue left out of the abridged version, favourite characters came vividly to life. Herbie's renditions of Blind Pew, complete with sinister cockney accent, plus Ben Gunn with his high pitched "Cheese I likes ...." were the highlights.

In fact it went so well that, when the BBC subsequently serialised a new adaptation of Stevenson's Kidnapped, Hawkesbury School invited the duo back for another rendition.

Sadly, Herbie passed away in 2006 but his place has been taken by Trustee Bill Fairney, whose goatskin costume has to be seen to be believed!

To the Hesitating Purchaser

This booklet has been produced to help support a campaign being led by the Long John Silver Trust to create a Bristol Treasure Island Trail. The Trustees are a group of local individuals who believe passionately in the project and the benefits it could bring to both Bristol and the South West, and have worked hard to form the Trust and achieve Registered Charity status.

Our aims are to commission, erect and maintain an iconic sculpture of Long John Silver, one of Bristol's most famous fictional characters, and establish a Treasure Island Trail of sculptures along the waterfront from King Street to Prince Street Bridge (where currently there are no waterside sculptures). We want the Trail to be enjoyed by people on foot or afloat, and also to tell the story in sequence, so careful thought has been given to their positioning. To make the Trail even more educational and inclusive we would also like to commission a "Pirate Boat" that will enable parties of school children and disabled people to experience the story of Treasure Island in a unique way.

To do this the Trust proposes seven sculptural works of art, which will cover all the principal events and characters from the classic novel. In the meantime, the trail has been laid out in this book and we hope it will be followed and enjoyed by many. We are actively pursuing the production of Plaques of the characters for each station of the Trail and once the Trail is complete we would also like to engage with Bristol's Performing Arts Schools to help bring the concept to life. We also would like to see Redcliffe Caves become an Interpretation Centre for the history of piracy and privateering in Bristol and the South West.

Apart from showing the initial thinking behind the Trail, this book explores some of the characters from Bristol's 300 year privateering past and their influence on writers such as Daniel Defoe and Robert Louis Stevenson. For 2008, which is the 125th Anniversary of Treasure Island's publication and the 300th Anniversary of Woodes Rogers' epic voyage, the Trust commissioned an eight-foot wicker sculpture of Long John Silver by Stephen Froome.

The Mervyn Peake Trust

When Bristol City Council launched the Great Reading Adventure in 2003, they produced an excellent booklet that showed the work of nearly every illustrator that ever worked on Treasure Island. By far the most dramatic and memorable of all these images were those done by Mervyn Peake. These provided the inspiration for the foundation of the Long John Silver Trust, so that when a Treasure Island Trail was first proposed, Mervyn Peake's illustrations immediately came to mind, paving the way for a feasible interpretation of the book in sculpture form.

When further looking into the accomplishments of Mervyn Peake it became instantly apparent that the man was a genius. Not only was he a great illustrator; he was an artist, poet and novelist, famed for his Nonsense Poems and other children's books, most notably Gormenghast.

The Trust contacted Mervyn's son, Sebastian, who shares his father's admiration for Robert Louis Stevenson and Treasure Island and is a most enthusiastic supporter of the Treasure Island Trail. Sebastian and the Mervyn Peake Trust have very generously allowed us to use some of those glorious illustrations in this book.

Sebastian told us that as a young boy in Sark, just after the war, he was used as Jim Hawkins' model, vividly recalling posing on the kitchen table in winter with just a smelly old oil stove for warmth. Another memory was his father's ability to quote verbatim any passage requested from Treasure Island.

The proposed 'coming to life' of Stevenson's wonderfully colourful characters in a sculpture trail for the city's harbour side has the enthusiastic backing of the Mervyn Peake family and Trust. We hope that the concept will be equally inspirational to others, and provide a lasting tribute to perhaps the best children's story ever written.

🏴 Long John Silver Trust

The Trust has formed strategic alliances with the following :-

Wickwar Brewery
Bristol Books and Publishers
PROPS (Providing Opportunities and Support)
The Bristol Rotary Breakfast Club
Bristol Radical History Group
Robert Louis Stevenson Club
Destination Bristol

Acknowledgements

Grateful Thanks are due to the following for their help, support and enthusiasm:

Bristol Evening Post	Redcliffe Press
Radio Bristol	Akeman Press
Jungle Talk	Bristol Record Office
Bristol Savages	Bristol Central Library
Bristol CAMRA	Sarah Larter
Bristol Ferry Boat Co.	Bristol's Festival of Ideas
Matthew Project	Broadcast Books

A big *Thank You* to all the Friends of the Long John Silver Trust
for their valued help and loyal support.

Nicholas Pocock's *A View from Sea Banks towards St Mary* **painted in 1781**

Pocock was a Bristol sea captain and Britain's first great maritime artist.

What is a Pirate?

What do we think of when we hear the word 'pirate'? A picture-book blackguard, complete with cutlass and Jolly Roger? Piracy must be one of the oldest crimes, and a pirate is actually anyone who robs or plunders at sea, or sometimes from the shore.

Since at least the 19th century, pirates have been recognized as "hosti humanis generis" (enemies of the human race). It is not often realized that piracy is still going on in many parts of the world, and, far from going away, is actually on the increase. Unlike the old time pirates, most of today's pirates get about in nippy speedboats. They're more likely to be wearing balaclavas than bandannas, and using AK- 47 assault rifles rather than cutlasses.

Piracy upon the high seas today is a prosecutable offence under international law. Seaborne piracy against merchant vessels remains a great problem particularly in the waters between the Pacific and Indian oceans, and specifically in the straits of Malacca and Singapore, which are used by over 50,000 commercial ships a year, the Red Sea and along the East Africa coast. Ships docking at Avonmouth and Portbury today may very well have experienced piracy attacks or threats when passing through these perilous waters.

For a long time the prosecution of piracy was a tricky business. Piracy on the high seas is not within the legal jurisdiction of any state. This means that countries can technically only prosecute any pirates they catch not on behalf of themselves, but for the 'common good'. In practice however, just as in centuries before, a country will only go to the trouble of prosecuting pirates if their own ships are being threatened.

Piracy and the West Country

The West Country has had links with piracy for at least 1000 years. The first mention of acts of piracy seems to have been in 915, when a Viking raid from Brittany sailed into the Bristol Channel and ravaged Herefordshire, until they surrendered to the Saxons. Guards were set on the South coast from Cornwall to the Avon to prevent the Vikings from landing, and they were forced to remain on Flatholme, many starving to death, until a favourable wind allowed them to escape to Ireland. In 1068.

Another raid of Vikings came from Ireland into the mouth of the Avon, rowing up to Bristol. However the Bristolians repulsed them and they sailed away again.

Pirates on Lundy

The next major spate of piracy in the South West was headed by Sir William de Marisco, who murdered a king's messenger at his manor at Portishead in 1235. He was outlawed and escaped to Lundy Island, which his family owned. Lundy was to have a regular and ever-changing pirate population: Marisco's descendents ravaged the ships of the Bristol channel for the next century, until the clan leader was finally captured by the soldiers of Henry III and dragged at the end of a horse's tail to Bristol and then on to London, where he was executed as a traitor. In the 1440s Colyn Dolphyn, a Breton pirate, used Lundy as a base until finally he ran ashore in Glamorgan and was executed by being buried up to his neck in Tresilian Sands near St Donats.

During the 16th and 17th centuries, Lundy was used as a base by Barbary Corsairs from North Africa. They were pioneered by Murat Rais, an Albanian known for his ferocity, who had been elevated to "Captain of the Seas" by the Sultan of Algiers. Murat Rais led his Corsairs out of their former stronghold in the Mediterranean up the coast of France and into the Bristol Channel, taking a heavy toll on the ships plying between Bristol, Ireland and the West Indies. Many English people were carried off as slaves to row their galleys home to North Africa. On the other side of the coin any captured Corsairs would be brought to Bristol and chained to the harbour wall at the Gib Tayler, a large dockside crane opposite the Ostrich pub, and left to drown as the incoming tide crept up the walls.

However the criminal activity was not all one way: The sailors of Bristol and the South West have themselves had a long history of shady dealings. To avoid the government's heavy import duties on luxury goods such as tobacco and rum, smuggling was for a long time a normal way of doing things for Bristol merchants. They would keep two sets of books; one for goods upon which duty had been paid, and one for the contraband, and a smuggler might readily cross the line from smuggling to piracy. Government officials trying to catch the smugglers red-handed in their activities on the lonely coasts of Somerset and North Devon were extremely unpopular with the locals, as whole communities benefited from the trade in contraband.

Spanish Galleon: 500 tons, 18 guns, strong, fast and manoeuverable. The Manila galleons, as classed by Rogers, could be up to 2000 tons.

The Prey: a *Merchantman*, 280 tons, 20 crew, 4 guns.

Age of Piracy in the Caribbean 1690-1718

Brigantine: 150 ton, 100 crew, 10 cannon. Popular with pirates; the Navy used them too. They could also be rowed with sweeps (oars) through the gunports if becalmed.

Schooner: 100 ton, narrow hull, shallow draft, 8 cannon, 75 crew, 4 swivel guns, 11 kts. Popular with pirates in the caribbean and N America.

Sloop: 100 tons, 8ft draft, 11 kts, 14 cannon, 75 crew, fast and shallow - drafted, an ideal pirate vessel.

Mervyn Peake's illustration of Jim Hawkins defending himself from the pirate Israel Hands

A Pirate's Vocabulary.

Buccaneer   This comes from *"boucan"*, a wooden frame which was used for cooking meat by hunters in the Caribbean. They became known as as boucaniers and when they took to piracy, took the name with them.

Corsair   This name derives from the Latin word *"Cursa"* means a raid, or expedition. These pirates, operating mostly in the Mediterranean, included the Moslem Barbary corsairs from the North African coast, with their strongholds in Tunis, Tripoli and Algiers. They operated from the times of the Crusades until 1816, when the bombardment of Algiers saw the last of them. The most famous Barbary Corsair was Barbarossa.

There were also Christian corsairs who operated out from Malta from the times of the Crusades onwards, 'legitimised' by "letters of marque" issued by the Knights of St John. Any Muslim Turks captured by the Christian Corsairs were forced into the hellish life of rowing the galleys of the Knights of St. John as slaves. It required 1000 slaves to man all the galleys of the Order, making Malta a veritable slave market until well into the eighteenth century.

Freebooter   This was another word for pirate, and derives from the Dutch word *"vrijbuiter"* - *vrij* meaning free and *buit* meaning booty.

Pirate   This comes from the Latin *"pirata"*, which means to attack, or assault.

Privateer   These men would carry a "letter of marque" from their governments, giving them permission to attack vessels belonging to the nation named in the letter, and, importantly, granting them immunity from punishment. The immunity conferred by such a letter, should the privateer be captured was, of course, questionable. Granting of "letters of marque" enabled a country to wage covert warfare. Sir Francis Drake, a famous privateer, was considered by the Spanish to be nothing but a pirate.

Instructions for privateers were issued by the Government and affected all such matters as manning and equipment, wearing of colours, conduct towards neutrals, procedure as to prize, ransom, disposal of prisoners, etc. Every commander had a copy of these instructions, and he was bound by them to render a copy of his journal to the Secretary of the Admiralty. Because the sailor crew were entitled to a share of the prize money - far more than a sailor could expect in wages from the navy - they did not need to be 'press-ganged', in fact a privateer could usually have his pick of sailors. Discipline was also less severe than in the navy, and often very slack indeed. As we will see from the adventures of Dampier, many a crew of privateers deserted their ships after losing patience at the non-appearance of a treasure ship whose booty they had been promised.

The Royal Navy of the early and mid18th century suffered low morale and poor leadership. An officer would be advanced by family influence, irrespective of any possible ability. A situation could and often did arise where a British merchantman (a private merchant's ship) might be taken by a French or American privateer, practically under the guns of the Royal Navy; while the more intrepid British privateers were taking the fight to the enemy in the anticipation of prizes.

Later in the century, there was a movement towards more able and humane leadership, exemplified by Admiral John Jervis, Lord St Vincent, who in turn encouraged famous admirals such as Nelson and Collingwood. By 1830, proper schemes for training the Royal Navy sailors were implemented, along with schemes for career advancement; and discipline became less brutal and arbitrary. This caused the use of the press gang to fall into disuse, though it was still legally sanctioned. With a more able and efficient Navy, the role of the privateers also became redundant.

Viking This derives from the Old Norse *"vik"*, meaning a creek or inlet, so a Viking was someone who haunted such places.

A Boucan, from which the buccaneers derived their name.

Captain Woodes Rogers and the Bristol Privateers

Bristol was a prominent port for privateering and many local people became wealthy through it. Privateers were supposed to have a licence (a letter of marque) that would allow them to attack ships and commerce belonging to a hostile nation. There is a fine line between being a pirate and a privateer and Captain Kidd, who lost his political masters in England and America who had originally sanctioned his Letter of Marque, was court-martialled for piracy and then horribly put to death.

In the early 17th century Bristol privateers were involved in the early colonisation of America and voyages of discovery, including some ill-fated searches for the North West Passage. Later privateers were extremely useful to the English government in actions against the French and Spanish, especially in the Caribbean.

One of the most successful privateers of all time was Captain Woodes Rogers. He was born in Bristol in 1679, the son of a successful sea captain. In 1708 he was made Commander of a sailing venture backed by the Bristol Corporation. Armed with a letter of marque which enabled him to legitimately attack Spanish and French ships, he sailed off down the coast of South America with fellow West Countryman Dampier as his pilot (navigator). They explored the Falkland Islands, rounded the Horn and nearly froze to death, then rescued the castaway Alexander Selkirk. After many successful raids on Spanish colonies where the ladies were liberated of their gold jewellery "in a most genteel manner", his little fleet of three ships returned home intact, with Woodes Rogers slightly less so: he had suffered a bullet in the mouth and a huge wooden splinter in his heel. Woodes Rodgers had became one of only three Englishmen to ever capture a Spanish treasure ship - an almost un-heard of feat - the others being Thomas Cavendish a century earlier and Lord Anson forty years later. Anson had a fleet of six naval ships and could only bring one home, making Woodes Rogers' achievement all the more remarkable.

The welcome home disintegrated into lawsuits, with many of his crew press-ganged onto other ships. Rogers even lost his home in Queen's Square for a while. It was to try and raise money that Rogers published a book based around his thrilling captain's log, *A Cruising Voyage around the World.* It became a bestseller, and inspired a host of similar adventure narratives. Woodes Rogers ended his eventful life as Governor of the Bahamas, which had become a virtual pirates' republic. He not only got the pirates pardoned by the Crown but persuaded them to fight off the Spanish, to make the colony succeed. He made many enemies and died mysteriously in 1732, possibly by poisoning. However, a grateful colony erected a statue to their governor, which stands in Nassau to this day.

Dampier, who had been Woodes Rogers' pilot, also published accounts of his buccaneering exploits. They were avidly read by the public, including both Daniel Defoe and Jonathon Swift. In fact Swift actually had Gulliver refer to Dampier as his cousin in his immortal classic, *Gulliver's Travels.*

It is widely known that Alexander Selkirk was rescued by Woodes Rogers and that his story was to be embellished into what could be called the first ever English novel, *Robinson Crusoe* by Daniel Defoe. What is not so well known is that Selkirk was also the inspiration for Robert Louis Stevenson's cheese-loving character, Ben Gunn. Another classic arising from Woodes Rogers' epic voyage, is Coleridge's *Rime of the Ancient Mariner.*

Bristol privateers continued to find fame and fortune on the high seas: one successful voyage in 1744 yielded so many prizes it needed 45 wagons loaded with treasure to transport it from Old Market Street to London. At its peak in the mid 1750s Bristol's privateers boasted around 40 ships, 7500 adventurers and between 1200 and 1400 guns.

Understandably, records on pirates and piracy are a little more obscure than those of their privateering cousins. Information usually came either from their victims or the pirates' pursuers. Captain Johnson (believed to be a pseudonym of Daniel Defoe) in his *General History of Ye Pyrates* gave graphic accounts and accurate statistics from both sources. For example, when talking about "Black Bart" Roberts - the famous Welsh pirate captain - he tells of the terrible fate that befell the African slaves that he had captured and the composition of his crew that ended up in Execution Dock

Interestingly, of the 53 men that were hanged on that occasion, 26 of them were from the West Country, including 6 from Somerset (two of whom were from Minehead) and 4 from Bristol. One of the most fascinating chapters in Johnson's book is his account of Blackbeard and his fiendish exploits, and it is no surprise to learn that Robert Louis Stevenson had a copy in his collection and equally that he chose to set *Treasure Island* in Bristol.

The following vignettes illustrate fully the rich and varied role Bristol played both in the factual and fictional story of pirates.

A CRUISING

VOYAGE

ROUND THE

WORLD:

First to the SOUTH-SEAS, thence to the EAST-INDIES, and homewards by the Cape of GOOD HOPE.

Begun in 1708, and finish'd in 1711.

CONTAINING

A JOURNAL of all the Remarkable Transactions ; particularly, Of the Taking of Puna and Guiaquil, of the Acapulco Ship, and other Prizes ; An Account of Alexander Selkirk's living alone four Years and four Months in an Island ; and A brief Description of several Countries in our Course noted for Trade, especially in the South-Sea.

With Maps of all the Coast, from the best Spanish Manuscript Draughts.

And an INTRODUCTION relating to the SOUTH-SEA Trade.

By Captain WOODES ROGERS, Commander in Chief on this Expedition, with the Ships Duke and Dutchess of Bristol.

LONDON, Printed for A. Bell at the Cross Keys and Bible in Cornhil, and B. Lintot at the Cross-Keys between the two Temple-Gates, Fleetstreet. M DCC. XII.

Edwin Russell's sculpture of Woodes Rogers stands on the site of Fort Nassau in the Bahamas, where Woodes Rogers had his headquarters when he was Governor. The sculpture was commissioned by Sir Henry Oakes for the British Colonial Hilton in the 1930s.

19

West Country Pirates and Buccaneers

"Admiral" Sir Henry Morgan
Buccaneer and Governor of Jamaica

Born in 1635 into a military family in Abergavenny, Wales, Morgan left school early and was shipped from Bristol to Barbados to become apprenticed as a cutler. Life as an indentured servant on the plantations did not agree with him and he escaped to serve as a subaltern on Cromwell's ship, the Western Design, which was part of Bristol Admiral William Penn's expedition that eventually conquered Jamaica in 1655.

Morgan turned buccaneer and the highlight of his career followed soon after, when he led a band of 2,000 English and French pirates in a raid on the rich Spanish-owned port of Panama. After sacking the city, Morgan returned to the Caribbean with a great treasure. He held a meeting of his fellow pirate kings on his flagship, HMS Oxford, but disaster struck when the vessel blew up, though sparing Morgan. The grateful Spanish attributed the event to the work of the statue of the Virgin Mary in Cartagena. Morgan was knighted by Charles II and appointed Lieutenant Governor of Jamaica. Under King's Orders, he turned on his former henchmen and associates in crime and hanged every pirate he could find.

Although he had a terrible reputation, Morgan became a respectable governor and died wealthy but childless in 1688. He had been a good administrator and founded the Jamaican town of Port Royal, which was destroyed in an earthquake a few years after his death.

William Dampier (1651 - 1715)

The extraordinary life of one of the West Country's most famous buccaneers, William Dampier, echoes both the personal and national greed which seems to have been prevalent throughout the late sixteenth century.

It was a time of a kind of high seas free-for-all - with the English navy hardly more governed by laws, or restraint, than the multitude of marauding pirates, buccaneers and privateers who sailed off in search of Spanish treasure ships.

Europe's main sea-faring nations - chiefly Holland, France, Spain and England - were bidding to acquire as many colonies as they could. These newly-acquired lands and ports, such as existed on the Caribbean islands and South American coast, were a tremendous temptation for every sort of adventurer and rogue and very vulnerable to pirate raids.

Dampier, born into a well off farming family in 1651 at East Coker, near Yeovil, was the second of six children. When he was eighteen he was apprenticed to a seaman at Weymouth. Because of his rural upbringing he was always interested in natural history and, during his first long voyage, made an early study of prevailing winds.

Although reputedly rather cowardly by nature, he saw action at sea in the Third Anglo-Dutch war in 1673, and afterwards worked on a Jamaican sugar plantation. But, after falling out with the plantation manager, he went back to sea and later to the Bay of Campeche, in the Caribbean swamps, to work as a logswood man, the trees being sent back to Europe as a valuable source of purple dye.

Dampier, now in his early twenties, was a faithful keeper of a journal of observations. He wrote a riveting account of the region's wildlife as well as about the wild behaviour of the "Baymen" - privateers no longer employed by the British government after a peace treaty with Spain.

These "Baymen" offered him a tempting lifestyle and, realising he could earn more from pillage than from log cutting, he joined a group who planned to raid the Mexican coastal towns. He returned to England in 1678, rich enough to wed - above his station it must be added - to Judith, a duchess's maid.

Dampier was too restless, however, to settle down to domestic life and he was soon back in pirate infested Jamaica where, after buying a small Dorset estate from a trader, he joined a newly formed buccaneer fleet. With the help of Mosquito Coast indians, this ruthless gang captured the port of Portobello and then, encouraged by the success of pirate Henry Morgan several years earlier, went on to attempt a raid on silver rich Panama city. This venture ended in failure, however; the fleet broke up and there was a mass defection of crew members.

William Dampier - buccaneer
An engraving of the original oil painting by Thomas Murray, 1697/8

A Ceawau

Contemporary illustration of a ship's worm of the sort that ate Dampier's ships. The only defence against these creatures was copper sheathing of the hull, hence "a copper-bottomed guarantee". However this often proved too expensive an investment for ships' owners.

Dampier, remaining on board ship, went on to join up with more French and English pirates. This bloodthirsty gang raided all along the Caribbean coast as well as Costa Rica, retreating periodically to the notorious buccaneer port of Tortuga.

After a quiet few months in Virginia the adventurer set off again, in 1683, on another raiding expedition. This time it was to be in the Pacific, and here he took careful naturalist notes of the islands of Juan Fernandez and the Galapagos. Hundreds of French and English freebooters joined the fleet and, rounding the Horn, they had yet another attempt at sacking Panama City, but were again repulsed, this time by Spanish warships.

Shortly afterwards Dampier joined the vessel *Cygnet* because, as his journal states, its captain, Edward Davis, would allow him to explore the Pacific. Davis had replaced Captain Swan, the original captain of the *Cygnet*. (Swan had been abandoned on a Philippine island with part of his crew after a mutiny). The plan was for Davis and Dampier to try and intercept one of the famed Spanish treasure galleons which sailed annually from Manila to Acapulco in Mexico. But they changed tack and, in 1686, decided to sail the 6000 miles from Mexico to Guam with a crew desperately short of rations.

This hunger must have made Dampier's descriptions of the exotic foods they found in Guam and the Philippines even more mouth watering. He was the first Englishman to give descriptions of breadfruit, bananas, and plantain.

For another year, the *Cygnet* sailed the South China seas and even landed briefly, in 1688, on the shores of Australia, then called New Holland - the first English ship to do so. Dampier was bitterly disappointed by the desert wastelands he found there - at great variance with the myth that had spurred him on - that of the wonderful new undiscovered continent, *Terra Australis Incognita*.

Leaving the *Cygnet* anchored at Great Nicobar Island, off the Indian coast, the adventurer then set off on a terrible 130 mile journey in an outrigger canoe, surviving dysentry and many other hazards, to finally arrive in Sumatra. For the next year and a half he explored Tonquin (it's now Vietnam), Malacca (now Melaka) on the Malay peninsula, and even India.

By the time that he eventually arrived home, in 1691, he had become first Englishman to have circumnavigated the globe since Thomas Cavendish, a century earlier.

Despite his adventures Dampier had not made his fortune; in fact his only possessions seem to have been his journal and a tattooed Philippino slave, 'Prince Giolo' - who died soon after going on show in London and Oxford. So, two year later Dampier was off once again, this time on a more lucrative quest. He was navigating The *Dove*, one of four ships looking for "trade" in the Caribbean.

Captain Kidd was a privateer armed with a letter of Marque entitling him to attack Spanish galleons. However he turned pirate when he went after an East Indiaman (a merchant ship). His political masters in England and America lost power and he was abandoned to the Execution Dock on charges of piracy. When Dampier was court-martialled he had to pass the swinging tarred corpse of Kidd each day: a fate that could so easily have befallen him as well.

A mutiny, however, soon turned the little fleet into a pirate one captained by Henry Avery. For once Dampier seemed to have been out of the action and he remained with The *Dove* at port in Spain, and even sued for back wages. However the High Court of Admiralty dismissed his claim and upheld the charge, that Dampier had abetted the mutiny, made by the fleet's owner. Realising that there was little loot coming his way, Dampier testified against six of his former shipmates when they were tried for piracy.

In 1697 the adventurer published A New Voyage Round the World, and later, by popular demand, a supplement to it. Full of blood-curdling accounts of piracy but noted more for its descriptions of the flora and fauna of the New World, the book was a great success, and Dampier found himself a popular hero, admired by merchants, statesmen, and scientists. He began to move in elevated circles and was even appointed to the well-salaried post of land-carriage man at the London Customs House. As an acknowledged expert he was called on to testify to the Board of Trade on piracy matters.

His reputation on a high, Dampier was, in 1699, given the command of *HMS Roebuck*. This was to be a scientific exploration of the Pacific plus a circumnavigation of Terra Australis but the navigator had to contend with a ship that was in a terrible condition, as well as having an inexperienced and unhappy crew.

One officer had so little respect for Dampier that he insulted him on several occasions - causing the short-fused captain to cane and then imprison him. The ship finally reached Australia but, as before, only touched it's barren northern shores before setting sail for New Guinea, hoping to round the continent that way. Dampier found a beautiful set of green islands - which he named New Britain - before being forced by the condition of his rotting ship to set sail for home.

But the *Roebuck* only made it as far as Ascension Island where, in 1701, the vessel sank. Dampier had to hitch a ride back to England aboard an East Indiaman (a fast sailing merchant ship), along with a cargo of forty Australian plants. They were taken to Oxford where they eventually formed the core of the Sheradian herbarium.

As a result of these voyages the adventurer is commemorated today in several Australasian place names: Dampier Strait, Roebuck Bay and Dampier Land in north West Australia, and the Dampier archipelago off the western coast.

When Dampier returned, in the summer of 1702, he had to face the disgrace of a court martial instigated by the officer he had mistreated. He was found unfit for naval command, but as he'd had enough of the slender pickings of a respectable life at sea, he didn't regard this as too much of a setback.

In September 1703 he sailed off on another prospective ambushing expedition to the Pacific with his sights again on the Spanish treasure galleon sailing out of Manila. He was, this time, commodore of a ship called the *St. George*,

Fitting out the DUKE and
DUCHESS in Bristol 1708
for Captain Woods Rogers
Expedition

— FRANK SHIPSIDES — 2004 —

The artist Frank Shipsides' impression of the *Duke* and *Duchess* being fitted out at Redcliffe Wharf, Bristol, for Captain Woodes Rogers' expedition around the world, which was piloted by Dampier.

accompanied by another, the *Cinque-Ports*. There is, unfortunately, no memoir of their unsuccessful, and shameful, attempt to ambush that elusive Spanish vessel. The disappointed sailors, who would have been given shares of the booty, all mutinied and deserted, with one departing crewman jeering "Poor Dampier, thy Case is like King James, every Body has left thee!" One of the unluckier mutineers was Scotsman **Alexander Selkirk**, cast off the *Cinque Ports* and marooned on Juan Fernandez island in November 1704. It would be many lonely years before he would be rescued by a later expedition led by Bristol seaman Woodes Rodgers and, ironically, Dampier himself.

Returning home in 1707 - after a brief stint in a Batavian prison on suspicion of piracy - Dampier had to face more allegations of ill temper, abuse of his officers, drunkenness, bribe taking and even cowardice (for refusing to board the Manila galleon) brought by his former crewmen, but astonishingly he was vindicated.

But, whatever his other failings, such was his reputation as a navigator that Dampier was recruited by Bristolian Captain Woodes Rogers for yet another privateering expedition. The plan was to take two ships, the *Duke* and the *Duchess*, and try and capture (yet again) the Manila galleon. But this time they were successful and Rogers returned to England in 1711 with a shipful of Spanish loot as well as the rescued castaway, Alexander Selkirk.

Dampier retired, initially a rich man, to London, but he was sued by the owners of the ships from his previous expeditions and died in November 1714, leaving debts of £677 17s. 1d. As his will made no provision for a wife, it's possible that she had pre-deceased him.

Contemporary, and later judgements on his turbulent, but interesting life, were quite kind. In Gulliver's Travels- inspired by Dampier's accounts of strange lands - the author Jonathan Swift wrote that he was an " honest man, and a good sailor, but a little too positive in his own opinions". The poet Coleridge praised his "exquisite mind' and much later another poet, John Masefield, delighted in his descriptions of natural history as the product of a "calm, equable, untroubled and delighted vision".

Dampier's writings certainly inspired a new genre of travel writing, taken up by both Daniel Defoe and Jonathan Swift in the early 18th century. These were followed later by the likes of Robert Louis Stevenson.

Dampier's acute observations of maritime climate, tides and compass variations proved invaluable to future generations of sailors and scientists. He has been credited with being the most important explorer - before Captain Cook - to inspire interest in the South Pacific. In recent times Dampier has even become recognised as a fore-runner of such luminaries as Charles Darwin, because of his acute observational and deductive skills.

Blackbeard 1680?-1718

Blackbeard's early life is shrouded in mystery. Academics argue over his birth place, birth date and even his original name, which has at least three variations: Edward Teach, Edward Thatch or even Edward Drummond. In Bristol his memory is a mixture of both denial and proud son but, despite this, local legend persists that he was born in Redcliffe. What is known isn't very savoury. He was thought to have 14 wives, but how many were "port wives" isn't clear. He served with Benjamin Hornigold and was given command of one of his prizes, a French slave ship named La Concorde which he renamed Queen Anne's Revenge (some pirates had Jacobite sympathies). He made the Bahamas his home during its "Pirate Republic" heyday, two years prior to Woodes Rogers' arrival. {Woodes Rogers' first task as Royal Governor was to clear out the nest of pirates]

Captain Johnson enjoyed describing Blackbeard, and the following description originates in his *"General History …"*. (Decency prevents the authors from using the anecdote regarding the pirate's last wife, a fifteen year old plantation owner's daughter.)

"Teach, the most colourful and well-known of all the pirates is a never dying legend. He was a massive man noted for his boldness, fiendish appearance and roguish ways. With cutlasses and three brace of pistols slung about him, he resembled a walking arsenal. His long black beard was twisted with brightly coloured ribbons and turned about his ears. Slow burning fuses (or matches) tucked under his hat wreathed his head with demonic smoke. All this, together with his fierce and wild eyes made him such a figure that imagination cannot form an idea of a fury from hell to look more frightful."

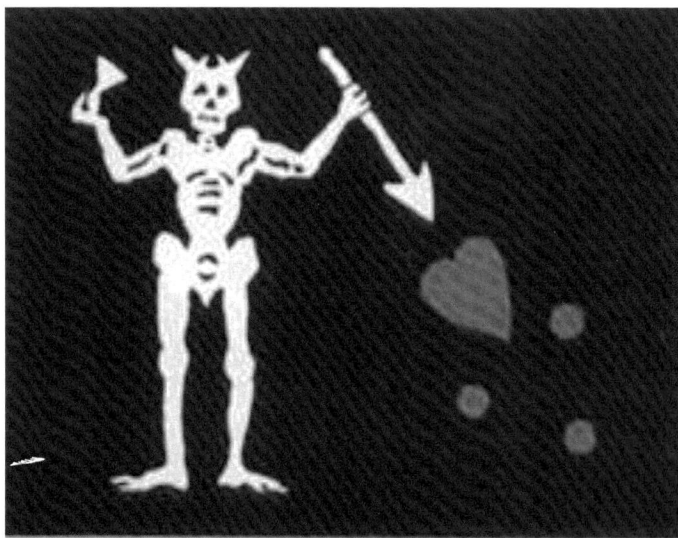

Blackbeard's Jolly Roger – a death figure with devils' horns, an hour glass (with time running out), and a pierced heart.

A rare, 1724, image of Blackbeard from Capt. Johnson's book, note the infamous '3 brace of pistols' and their early design (no proper handles).

One day at sea he said to a few of his men, "come, let us make a hell of our own, and try how long we can bear it." He took them below, closed up the hatches and set on fire several pots filled with brimstone and other acrid matter. One by one, close to suffocation, the men were forced to seek the upper deck. Blackbeard held out the longest and was quite pleased that he was better fitted to live in hell than the others.

On another cruise in the early 1700s Blackbeard punished a mutinous crew by marooning them on **Dead Man's Chest**, a small remote island in the British Virgin Islands chain, without water or landing places. Each was given a cutlass and a bottle of rum and Teach's hope was that they would kill each other, but when he returned at the end of 30 days he found that 15 had survived. This would explain in full the verse:

Fifteen men on the dead man's chest,
Yo ho ho ho, and a bottle of rum!
Drink and the devil had done for the rest,
Yo ho ho ho, and a bottle of rum!

This of course was immortalised in Stevenson's Treasure Island.

At the edge of the township in the Bahamas, Blackbeard held his court under a wild fig tree. He used to sit in council amongst his banditti, concerting or promulgating and exercising the authority of a magistrate. It is said that under the tree he kept a barrel of rum from which all who passed by were invited to drink. Those who hesitated were given a choice of drinking or being shot. Amazingly several wild fig trees grow today in Bristol, one of which is opposite the old Georges Brewery in Castle Park (actually growing out of the river wall).

Hornigold took Rogers' pardon in 1718, but Blackbeard carried on his reign of terror in Virginia. There, with his ship's master Israel Hands, they caused havoc all around: one of their more notorious acts was to blockade harbours for days on end to obtain goods and ransom money. In the end Governor Spottiswood brought in the Royal Navy to finish Blackbeard off.

Immediately prior to this, Israel and Blackbeard's pilot, Marshall, were drinking together, and without provocation Teach drew out a pair of pistols and cocked them under the table. When he was ready, he crossed them and fired. Hands was shot through the knee and so missed the last engagement. When asked why he had done this, Teach said, "Damn you all! Unless I now and then kill one of my men, they will forget who I am".

Blackbeard at Merchant's Landing overseas the highly-successful Bristol Festival of the Sea in 1996

The man sent by the Royal Navy to terminate Blackbeard's career was Lieutenant Robert Maynard in his sloop the Pearl, and on 22nd November 1718 Maynard tricked him into battle off Ocracoke. After a savage encounter, in which he sustained over 20 cuts and at least 5 shots, he was killed and decapitated. His headless body was thrown overboard and allegedly swam round his ship 3 times before disappearing. Of Maynard's men, 10 were killed and 24 were wounded.

As was the custom with a pirate, his head was hung from the bowsprit, and the skull ended up as a drinking vessel in a tavern in Williamsburg. The authorities caught up with Hands and would have hanged him as well had he not been reprieved at the last minute by a proclamation prolonging the pirates' pardon. He finished his days in London a poor lame beggar.

Alexander Selkirk

Marooned sailor Alexander Selkirk, who died in 1721, is thought by many to be the inspiration behind Daniel Defoe's classic novel *Robinson Crusoe*. Born and brought up in Largo, Fife, when he was seventeen Selkirk escaped the punishments of the Scottish kirk authorities for so called "indecent" behaviour in church by running away to sea. Returning six years later, however, he soon quarrelled with his family and, in 1703, left home, but not Largo, for good.

A capable sailor and navigator he was appointed master of the privateer *Cinque Ports* under Captain Charles Pickering. Together with another vessel, *The George*, commanded by West Countryman William Dampier, the two ships left for the South Seas.

Captain Pickering, unfortunately, died en-route and was succeeded by Captain Thomas Stradling. Although Selkirk proved himself a steady and reliable seaman, especially around Cape Horn, it is probable that he formed part of a subsequent mutiny when the men got to Juan Fernandez island, off the Chilean coast. The crews had been promised rich pickings from the heavily laden Spanish galleons plying that coast. But they continued to have little success and the two commanders quarrelled to such an extent that they eventually parted company.

Selkirk and Stradling, on the *Cinque Ports,* continued sailing on around the South American coast. Eventually Selkirk decided that the ship, and its commander, were completely unfit for the voyage and declared he would rather disembark at Juan Fernandez island, where they were berthed for a refit and to take on water, than sail on any further.

He was taken at his word and left the ship, according to Woodes' Rodgers account, with *"his Clothes and Bedding, with a Firelock, some Powder, Bullets, and Tobacco, a Hatchet, a Knife, a Kettle, a Bible, some practical Pieces, and his Mathematical Instruments and Books"*. The moment the vessel pulled away, however, he had a sudden change of heart and pleaded to be taken back on board. Stradling, fearing that he would lose this opportunity to get rid of the troublesome sailor, closed his ears and *the Cinque Ports* sailed off.

In his first few months on the island Selkirk went about distracted "and had much ado to bear up against melancholy, and the Terror of being left alone in such a desolate place". However, the onset of winter forced him to build two huts, and faced with the challenge of survival until picked up by a passing vessel he gradually became reconciled to his fate.

He studied his Bible and began a routine of daily exercises which included singing psalms and reading the scriptures aloud. It kept up his spirits and also helped him retain the use of his speech. And so he would know which day was the Sabbath (Sunday) he also kept a calendar. He bred cats, which as well as giving him some kind of company, preserved him from the rats which gnawed constantly at his feet and clothes as he slept.

His chief amusement was to hunt goats, but after exhausting all of his powder and shot he relied on fleetness of foot to capture them. He tamed the kids to ensure a continual source of food - after all, he thought, one day he might not be able to run after them.

In his account of the four years that he spent alone on the island, Selkirk stressed the importance of two incidents. The first occurred whilst he was out hunting. Having stalked a goat to an unfamiliar part of the island, he lunged to catch the animal and the momentum carried him over the edge of an unseen precipice. The fall knocked him unconscious for at least a day and when he recovered his senses he discovered the goat dead beneath him.

Second, he was very nearly captured by Spaniards who arrived at the island in two vessels. Anxious to find out the their nationality, Selkirk was inadvertently spotted from the ships. A landing party was dispatched, and several shots fired in his direction, but Selkirk's agility allowed him to hide in the branches of a tree as his pursuers searched for him beneath.

Then, in February 1709, two Bristol privateers, the *Duke* and *Duchess,* anchored at the island for water. The *Duke* was commanded by Captain Woodes Rogers with Dampier on board as pilot.

After dark Rogers spotted a light on the island and so, the next day, sent two boats to investigate. Towards evening one returned, together with *"a Man cloth'd in Goat-Skins, who look'd wilder than the first Owners of them [who] had so much forgot his Language for want of Use, that we could scarce understand him, for he seem'd to speak his words by halves".* The rescued man had been alone on the island for four years and four months.

Although no love was lost between them Dampier recommended Selkirk as the best man on the old *Cinque Ports* and Rogers appointed him as mate on the *Duke.* Both ships then sailed off to scour the coast of Chile. Within a month a prize ship was taken, and, renamed the *Increase,* Selkirk was appointed master.

Hoping to intercept vessels sailing between Panama and Lima, Rogers led them to the Galápagos Islands for refitting before taking up positions off Cape St Lucas to await the arrival of the Spanish galleon bound for Acapulco. Low on bread, and with worms penetrating deep into their vessels' sheathing, they were about to weigh anchor when at last, a Spanish sail was sighted. The Englishmen were in luck - they were able to seize the richly laden *Nuestra Señora de la Encarnación.*

When, early in 1710, Rogers set out to cross the Pacific, a voyage of over 6000 miles, his original ships were augmented by two others. The *Nuestra Señora,* renamed the *Bachelor,* had Selkirk appointed master under Captain Thomas Dover.

The Cock and Bottle Public-House, with Part of Messrs.
Ames and Gadd's Warehouses, Castle-Green, Bristol.

-"Nor leaves his Bottle till the Cock doth crow "

**During his time in Bristol, Selkirk stayed at the *'Cock and Bottle'* inn,
which was handy for the *'Star'* where he is said to have met Defoe.**

The little flotilla reached Guam in March and then left for Batavia - which they
sailed into in late June. Here they shared out a quantity of the booty, Selkirk
acting as a commissioner. His own share was eighty pieces of eight. Then, after
refitting at Horn Island, they sailed for the Cape of Good Hope where they
stayed for over three months.

34

A contemporary illustration of Defoe's Robinson Crusoe, which was inspired by the published adventures of Alexander Selkirk.

In April they sailed north in a convoy of twenty-five Dutch and English ships, arriving off the Shetlands in mid July. Selkirk arrived back in London in October 1711. His extraordinary circumnavigation had taken over eight years, more than half of which had been spent alone on his island.

Selkirk was feted, wined and dined after an account of his adventures was published by Rogers in *"A Cruising Voyage Round the World"* (1712). His rehabilitation, however, proved less successful. Coming to live in Bristol, possible with Woodes Rogers in Queen Square, we learn that an "Alexander Selkirke" of the parish of St Stephen, was wanted for an assault on Richard Nettle, shipwright, on 23 September 1713.

Some time later Selkirk returned to Largo as a recluse, constructing a cave in his father's garden. He became infatuated with a girl named Sophia Bruce, with whom, it appears, he eloped to London. It's even possible they married. In a will of January 1718, as he was about to leave, once more, for sea, Selkirk referred to Sophia as *"his loveing and well beloved friend Sophia Bruce of Pellmell London, Spinster"* and appointed her his executor and heir.

In October 1720 the sailor embarked on HMS Weymouth as master's mate and in December married a Plymouth widow called Frances Candis. He then made new will leaving everything to her. By March the following year the mariner was involved in operations against pirates on the Guinea coast and it was here, as other crew members fell sick, that he probably contracted the disease that was to kill him.

The Weymouth's log records Selkirk's death in December 1721. Then followed a legal battle over his estate between Frances Candis her new husband and his first wife Sophia. The latter's bid proved unsuccessful and her fortunes eventually sank so low that she was forced to beg for parish relief.

In 1866 a tablet in honour of Selkirk was placed near his lookout on Juan Fernandez island and a bronze statue, erected some twenty years later, stands on the site of his former home in Largo. His sea chest and a coconut shell cup, which he may have used on the island, are preserved in the national museums of Scotland.

But Selkirk's best memorial must surely be Daniel Defoe's portrait of the castaway, *Robinson Crusoe,* based on his life, which was published in 1719. There is some slight evidence that Defoe and Selkirk actually met, but stories that Defoe callously plundered Selkirk's journal for material, while telling its author it would never sell, are unlikely.

Two famous writers inspired by Pirate Tales

Daniel Defoe and the writing of Robinson Crusoe

Built over the old dungeons of Bristol's ruinous Norman castle, in long demolished Cock and Bottle lane, there once stood a famous old pub, the **Star Inn,** the haunt of many of the city's characters and "convivial wits". Could it be that, drinking and smoking amongst them, if only for a short while, was that famous writer, Daniel Defoe, pricking up his ears for likely material for a planned adventure yarn? It's very possible.

Defoe had been born in London in 1660, the son of a wealthy tallow merchant. Initially intended for the life of a non-conformist minister, rarely was there such a mismatch of occupation and character. Declaring that *"the pulpit is none of my office"* he followed his father into commerce, but a series of highly speculative ventures ended in financial disaster with Defoe owing his creditors thousands of pounds. He was never to be out of debt for the rest of his life and wrote really to try and earn a crust.

As well as being a struggling entrepreneur, Defoe was also pamphleteer - he hated religious intolerance - a journalist, poet, spy and double agent, and a revolutionary dreamer. During his life he published well over 300 works.

For much of his remarkable life he was haunted by his creditors and by the mobs who, incensed by the content of his political pamphlets, wanted to lynch him. He was imprisoned four times. On the other hand there were periods of high favour when King William I and his court treated him like a celebrity.

While writing an account of his journeyings through southern England, Defoe ended up in hiding in Bristol, on the run once more from his London creditors. He became known as the *"Sunday Gentleman"* - due to his habit of only daring to show himself in public on Sundays - when no lawyer or creditor could serve legal papers on him. He struck a dashing figure, "accoutred in the fashion of the times, with a fine flowing wig, lace ruffles and a sword by his side".

Contemporary reports also mention that a drinking companion of his at the time was Alexander Selkirk (aka *Robinson Crusoe*), the Scottish castaway who had achieved a measure of fame some years before through the best-selling narrative of the Bristol privateer, Captain Woodes Rogers. Selkirk lived up to his fame by his habit of walking the streets clothed in his goat skins. Sworn affidavits of the period insist that *"Selkirk placed his papers in Defoe's hands and that from them he wrote Robinson Crusoe".* Defoe, however, denied ever meeting either Selkirk, Woodes Rodgers, or that other famous West Country

Daniel Defoe

sea dog and travel writer, William Dampier, dismissing them all *as "illiterate sailors."* Nevertheless, it seems beyond doubt that his story of castaway Robinson Crusoe is based on the life of Selkirk.

Robinson Crusoe was published in April 1719 when he was about fifty-nine. Although read nowadays as an extraordinary, but straightforward, account of a castaway's amazing survival on a remote desert island, in its time the book was intended as a kind of lecture on Defoe's theories of government and religion. It was a plea for Britain's settlement and domination of new lands to be by trade rather than by military might.

Defoe was saying that English settlers could grow their coffee, spices and other crops just as effectively in Africa, only two weeks away by sail, rather than the Caribbean, a perilous ten weeks' sail away through pirate infested waters. He complained that the natural riches of soil and climate were going to waste. Even the lazy Portuguese, Defoe reminded his readers, had got around to growing coffee in Brazil.

The two best-selling publications in those days were sermons and travel books, so Defoe had not misjudged his audience. The book sold out and was then reprinted twice within two months. Defoe published a sequel and by the end of the year the two parts were published together, along with a map and six illustrations.

A year later and the story had been translated into French, Dutch and German. Although the author died of a stroke in 1731, penniless and *"sinking under the Weight of "Insupportable Sorrows"*, ***Robinson Crusoe*** has earned him the title of *"The father of the English Novel."*
The book, never out of print since its publication, has inspired a host of imitations. It was, without doubt, one of the inspirations for Robert Louis Stevenson's classic adventure yarn, Treasure Island.

A 'wanted' poster for Daniel Defoe of 1704.

"That fools look out, and knaves look on."

St. James', January 10th, 1704.

Whereas Daniel Defoe, *alias* Daniel De Fooe, is charged with writing a scandalous and seditious pamphlet, entitled *The Shortest Way with Dissenters*. He is a middle-sized, spare man, about 46 years old, of a brown complexion, but wears a wig; a hooked nose, a straight chin, gray eyes, and a mole near his mouth. A reward of £50 is offered for his apprehension.

Robert Louis Stevenson and the writing of *Treasure Island*

The stirring pirate tale, **Treasure Island** by Robert Louis Stevenson, must surely rate as one of the greatest adventure stories ever written. *" If this don't fetch the kids"* he was to write, *"Why, they have gone rotten since my day!"*

As far as the author was concerned these terrifying tales of lawless pirates and buccaneers had only come to an end a century or so previously. Although Stevenson originally intended the book for a young audience, and even dedicated it to his young step-son, the book was an immediate success with readers of all ages.

Stevenson's had been a lonely and sickly childhood. The son of a Scottish lighthouse engineer and his wife, who was a rigid Calvinist, he was born in Edinburgh in 1850. His mother read him Shakespeare and the Bible and his devoted nurse fired his imagination with lurid anti-Papist tales. It was these influences that turned Stevenson into a passionate advocate of religious and cultural freedom, and his subsequent adventures as a young man certainly tested the moral tolerance of his parents. A family saga that also influenced him greatly was the fate of his two uncles - they had died trying to reclaim money and property out of which they had been swindled on the Caribbean island of St. Kitts.

The young Stevenson had a lot of time to read, and it was the popular travel narratives of the day that were to prove a direct inspiration for *Treasure Island* and its vivid descriptions of the seafaring life. Often written by retired sea-farers, these were personal accounts of exploration in distant exotic lands coupled with blood-curdling escapades. They proved extremely popular and excited the public's curiosity about the barely explored new lands of the Americas and East Indies.

The most well-known of these accounts were written by the Somerset-born privateer, navigator and naturalist, William Dampier, and by Captain Woodes Rodgers, who lived in Bristol's Queen's Square in the early eighteenth century, and who set sail from Bristol's docks to engage in privateering (which was, in effect, government-sanctioned raids on Spanish treasure ships). These men, sometimes employed by the government, more often than not sought personal wealth through this type of licensed piracy. They survived the extreme dangers of sea battles and raids, as well as the many perils of disease and starvation that went with their life styles.

As explorers they made meticulous observations on the climates, currents, winds and tides of those new regions whose wealth they, or others, hoped to exploit. Their accounts, without doubt, provided Daniel Defoe with the inspiration to write ***Robinson Crusoe,*** published in 1719, a book certainly read by the young Stevenson.

Robert Louis Stevenson in Davos, Switzerland, at the time of writing *Treasure Island* in 1881.

Stevenson, having survived his own childhood perils, grew into a flamboyant and non-conformist young man, reluctantly studying, at his father's insistence, the law. He was quite tall but very thin, suffering intermittently from a tuberculosis-like illness which was often to threaten his life. His many friends loved him for his vitality, charm and brilliant conversation as he paced ceaselessly to and fro, constantly smoking cigarettes.

He sometimes wore a dark blue pirate cloak fastened with a snake buckle, and spent the little allowance his parents gave him in the brothels and low life taverns of Edinburgh, *"in the companion of seamen, chimney sweeps and thieves"*, as he put it, which must have furnished abundant inspiration for the gallery of roguish characters he was to later create.

Whilst still in Edinburgh Stevenson got to know a one-legged Gloucestershire poet called William Henley, who had come to the city to seek medical advice from the famed Dr Lister and to try and save his leg from the ravages of TB. They became good friends with Stevenson saying, *"there is something boisterious and piractical in his manner of talk... he will roar you down.. he will undergo passions of revolt and agony"*. In short, he was to become the template for the fictitious Long John Silver.

Needless to say his law studies did not survive long, although, in 1875, he did actually get called to the Bar. Three years later, to his father's great disapproval, he sailed to America to marry the love of his life, a divorced mother of two, Fanny Osborne.

His shocked parents, eventually reconciled to the match - and to the fact that their son was now devoted to the writing of horror and adventure tales rather than practising at the Bar - promised him an annual income of £250. Stevenson and his family (which now included a twelve year old stepson, Lloyd) returned to Scotland, where, encouraged by his magnanimous father, he began to write **Treasure Island** in 1881.

Stevenson, however, had been diagnosed with TB and it was recommended that he go to a Swiss clinic. Here he met John Addington Symonds the Bristol writer and historian, (the gifted son of Dr Symonds a famous surgeon), who was to have a great influence upon him and whose character he was to celebrate in print. Could it be that whilst conversing with Symonds he began to toy with the idea of setting his yarn in Bristol - as well as using the names Trelawny and Smollett, both associated with the city.

At first the adventure story was serialized in a boy's magazine, **Young Folks** - under the pseudonym Captain George North - between October 1881 and January 1882. It only earned it's author, as he was to put it, *"one hundred jingly jangly pounds"* and initially attracted little attention.

However, when Stevenson revised it and published it in book form a year later, it captured the public's imagination. Since then it has never since been out of print and has been translated into many languages. There have been plays,

The frontispiece of the *Silverado Squatters* written in California before *Treasure Island*. The hero, Juan Silverado, was the inspiration for the name John Silver.

films, television and radio adaptations, sequels, and even musicals, as well as notable illustrated editions.

Stevenson, who went on to write many more tales, travelled widely. He and Fanny eventually ended up on the island of Samoa on a plantation 600 feet above sea level, where he lived like a chieftain surrounded by his family and servants in a magnificent house designed by himself.

The author was known for his great hospitality and his visitors included missionaries, officials, officers from British warships and traders, plus Samoan chiefs and their retainers. These last gave him the name *Tusitala*, meaning Writer of Tales. When he died on December 3rd, 1884, forty Samoans cut a steep path up the mountainside and buried him, as he had wished, on the summit of Mount Vaea, where a memorial stands over his grave to this day.

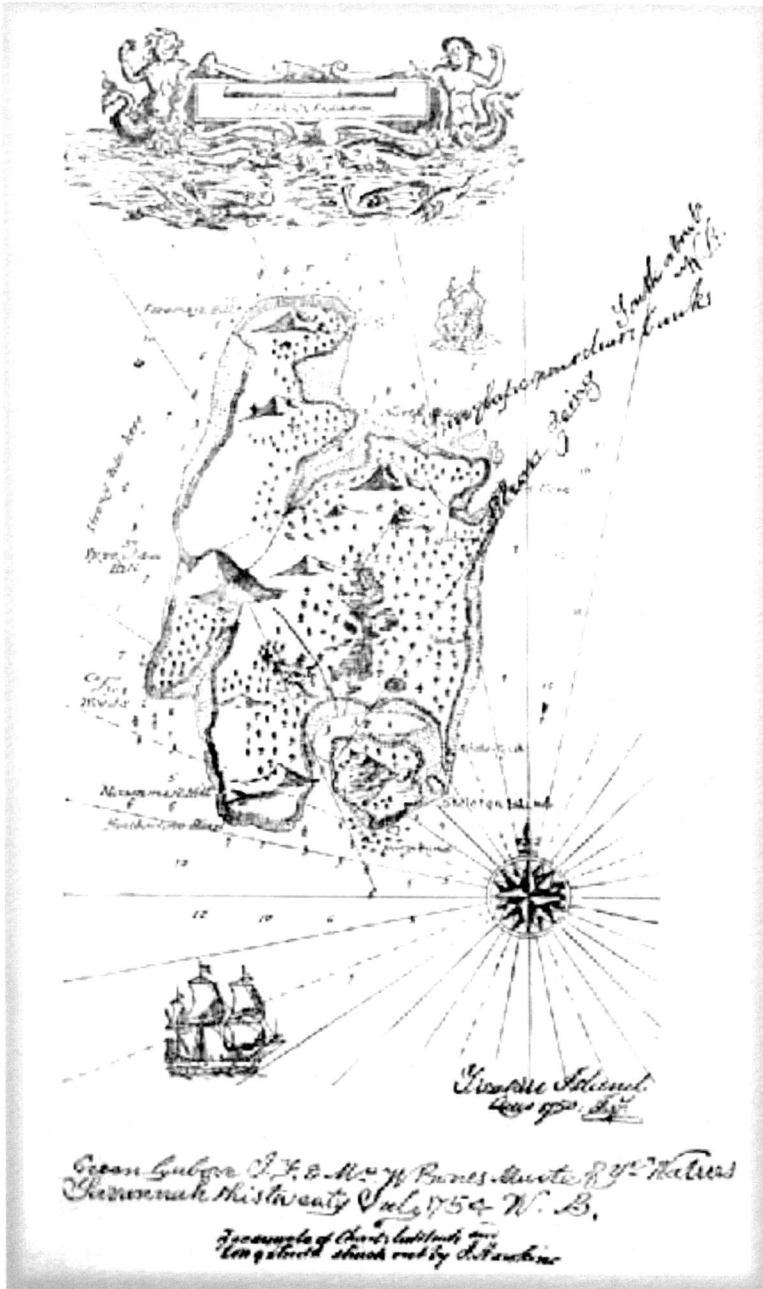

The map that started it all. After two weeks of torrential rain in Braemar, Scotland, Stevenson and his father drew this treasure map to amuse themselves. From this Robert Louis Stevenson created Treasure Island itself. In "fifteen glorious days" half of the book had been written.

John Addington Symonds of Clifton Hill House, a famous Bristol historian and classicist, friend of Robert Louis Stevenson. On long cold winter nights he spoke of his home town to Stevenson, which possibly inspired him to make Bristol part of the setting of *Treasure Island*.

Bust of William Ernest Henley by Auguste Rodin. Stevenson based the character of Long John Silver on Henley.

♟ Long John Silver Trust

The Objectives
The Trust has been formed to create an innovative sculpture of fiction's most famous rascal (he also happens to be Bristol's most famous pub landlord).

This has evolved into a revolutionary idea for a further six artworks around Bristol's ancient harbour that will bring to life Stevenson's classic novel *Treasure Island – The Bristol Treasure Island Trail.*

To help fulfil our Charity Commission obligations, we want to be both inclusive and educational and this has led to one of our most satisfying alliances with **PROPS.**

Another of our aims is to connect with Bristol's Pirate and Privateering maritime past. Partly because of these, the 18th Century was Bristol's "Golden Age" but there is very little left in the city to remind us of this.

From *Neptune* to *Nipper*, Bristol has some great Public Art, but apart from the statues of *John Cabot* and the *Elizabethan Seamen* (outside the Council House) and the bust of *Samuel Plimsoll*, there's very little to show of Bristol's nautical past.

Hence our Trail, which will make more of the city's old dockside and inns, an area currently bereft of any Public Art. **The Trail** will tell Stevenson's classic in sequence around the **Floating Harbour,** becoming one of the best tourist attractions around.

Just as RLS started *Treasure Island* with a map, so we started the Trail, using Bristol's two rivers, **Queen Square**, ancient caves, **Port Wall** and **St Mary Redcliffe Church.** We were on our way, adding elements from the original map such as the compass rose, sailing ship and scale of miles.

It's our intention to make the Trail permanent with **Pavement Plaques**, and if these prove popular, follow them up with the sculptures. To help achieve this, **Sebastian Peake** has graciously allowed us to use silhouettes from his father's work and we will combine these with our map icon. Plaque designer **Mike Baker** of Living Easton fame has been lined up to make them a reality.

The ultimate objective of the Trust is to raise sufficient funds to commission a statue of *Long John Silver* himself, to stand in front of *'The Spyglass'* inn, generally thought to be based on **'The Hole in the Wall'** in Queen's Square.

Bristol Treasure

Treasure Island Trail

Bristol 2008

A. Blind Pew
B. The Captains Papers
C. Long John Silver
D. Jim Hawkins
E. Ben Gunn

Bristol Bridge

Baldwin Street

King Street

Walsh Back

Island Trail

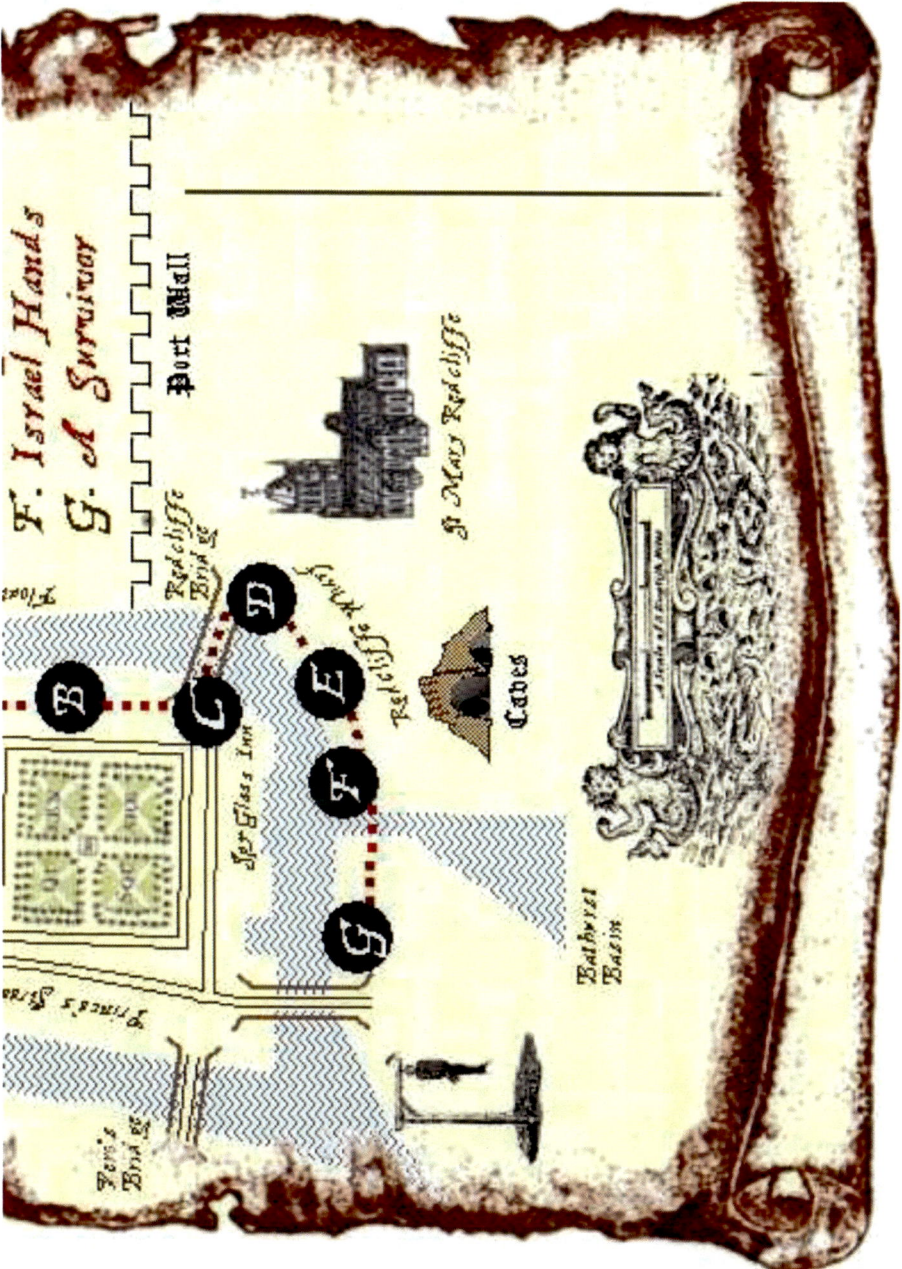

Blind Pew and Jim **Mervyn Peake, 1949**

The Bristol Treasure Island Trail

Blind Pew

The opening chapters of **Treasure Island** are set on the Devon coast at an inn called The *Admiral Benbow,* where young Jim Hawkins lives with his parents. The remoteness of the place attracts an old sea dog by the name of **Billy Bones** who, as it turns out, possesses a map showing the whereabouts of Cap'n Flint's treasure. Pirates up and down the coast are searching for him and one such fellow, **Black Dog**, eventually finds him.

After this rum-sodden Billy begins to confide in Jim. Then another pirate, *Blind Pew*, arrives on the scene, and when he hands Billy the infamous **Black Spot**, a sign that his days are numbered, the shock is enough to kill him. Before he dies however, and just before Blind Pew returns with his pirate band, he thrusts the treasure map into Jim's hands.

By now the lad had fortunately summoned help. Two mainstays of the community, Dr Livesey and Squire Trelawney with his men, turn up in the nick of time and set to with the pirates. Then, in the confusion that follows, Blind Pew is trampled to death.

*The Trust has chosen **King St.** for the start of the Bristol Treasure Island Trail because it's considered to be Bristol's most historic and atmospheric street. It not only contains Britain's oldest continuously working theatre, but it is also blessed with two ancient hostelries, both renowned for their sea-going associations - **The Naval Volunteer** and the **Llandoger Trow.***

The Captain's Papers **Mervyn Peake, 1949**

𝕭 *The Captain's Papers*

After the pirates have been scattered Jim admits to his rescuers what they have been searching for. Using the pirate map Squire Trelawney immediately starts to make plans to set sail and retrieve the treasure. Dr Livesey is concerned because the Squire is not known as a man who can keep a secret. The three then set off for Bristol Docks to find a ship.

Here, Dr Livesey's fears are confirmed. Despite securing a worthy ship -*The Hispaniola* - and engaging a good captain called Smollett, the Squire starts blabbing their plans around town. He then employs, as crew, a sea cook and - although he is unaware of it at the time - a pirate, by the name of Long John Silver. Much against Captain Smollett's wishes, Silver gets more and more of his old desperados on board as crew.

*Half way along Bristol harbour's **Welsh Back**, between **King Street** and
The Hole in the Wall pub, there is an opening amongst the dockside buildings
where the officers of **the Hispaniola** would possibly have planned their voyage.
This would have been done by many seafarers in this locality. This is also
where merchant and seaman Woodes Rogers who lived in **Queen Square**,
along with Bristol physician and second captain, Dr. Thomas Dover and West
Country pilot William Dampier, would have fitted out their vessels, the Duke
and Duchess, for their successful privateering trip to the Pacific in 1708.*

Long John Silver **Mervyn Peake, 1949**

C *Long John Silver*

Silver's Bristol dockside pub was the ***Spy-Glass Inn*** - and Jim was to meet him there. He recoils with horror when he discovers that the landlord has only one leg. Could this be the man, he thinks, that he was warned about?

The jovial Silver gets on well with just about everybody and before long not only has he befriended Jim but Trelawney has confided in him as well. The lad is fascinated by Silver's parrot, Cap'n Flint, who cries out *"Pieces of Eight, Pieces of Eight"*.

Despite Jim spotting Black Dog in the ***Spy-Glass***, he remains unaware of Silver 's dark side. The cook's choice of crew leads to a row between Cap'n Smollett and Squire Trelawney. The Captain says that he doesn't like the sound of the voyage OR the crew and that everyone in the port, except him, seems to know their destination. Cautious Smollett eventually puts to sea with firearms locked in the aft cabin.

*Many a Bristol inn has laid claims to be the **Spy-Glass**, but the only surviving pub that really fits the description is* Queen Square's ***The Hole in the Wall.*** *Situated on the quayside, with an entrance from different streets and even possessing its very own spy-hole feature, originally used as a look-out for the hated press gang, the pub offers everything, even a view across the river to* ***Redcliffe*** *where he was born.*

Jim in the apple barrel **Mervyn Peake, 1949**

Jim Hawkins

The ship sets sail with Mr Arrow, the first mate, suspicious of Silver and his cronies. He gives them a hard time and Long John has a job keeping the crew's tempers at bay, telling them that he is going to "take care" of Arrow.

He tempts the first mate with Plum Duff, complete with a double dose of rum. He then plies him with extra tots and during a storm he is washed overboard. The piratical crew are still not happy and plan to mutiny - but their plans are overheard by Jim while he is hiding in an apple barrel.

After land is sighted, Jim informs the squire, the doctor and the captain about the planned mutiny. The Squire realises just what a bad judge of character he's been.

Silver is in a long boat towing the Hispaniola to a safe anchorage when the pirates attack the officers. Silver calls one of the pirates, George Merry, "a blundering squid" for disobeying his orders.

Alongside **Redcliffe Wharf,** *by the bridge, and set amongst the dockside cobbles and hoists, the Trust would like to see a statue of Jim resting against some apple barrels and keeping a weather- eye out for rascally Long John Silver. Using barrels would echo the days of Bristol as a working port.*

Ben Gunn meets Jim **Mervyn Peake, 1949**

E **Ben Gunn**

Just as the pirates gain the shore Jim runs away and escapes. He then runs into the marooned Ben Gunn who is frightened of Flint's men - and Long John Silver in particular. He tells Jim that, although he has stayed alive on goats and berries, he longs for some cheese. When Gunn realises that the lad isn't one of Flint's men they became friends and Gunn shows him a coracle he had made.

Meanwhile the Squire and the others have left the ship for the shore, leaving two men on board to keep the pirates out. But they were soon overpowered and the mutineers start firing on the Squire's party. They make their way to an old stockade where Jim is reunited with them and prepare to repel the inevitable pirate attack. Silver - after unsuccessfully attempting a truce - calls out "them that die'll be the lucky ones!". Smollett and some others attempt to chase off the pirates but receive shots in exchange. Several men on both sides are killed.

The men in the stockade are concerned that the pirates may bring up the Hispaniola and flatten the stockade with cannon fire. Without telling anyone Jim goes back to the Hispaniola, using Gunn's coracle, to stop them.

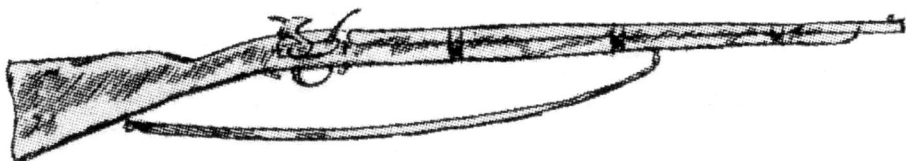

Redcliffe Caves - *one of Bristol's hidden treasures - have had many uses over the centuries and would be the natural haunt of someone like Gunn, emulating his cave-like home on* **Treasure Island**. *The caverns, which have spawned many legends - ranging from King Alfred's 9th century hideout to associations with smugglers and slaves, were mostly formed by the excavation of sand for the making of bottle glass during the 17th and 18th centuries. The sand was also used as ship's ballast and the caves as general storage by African traders.*

Israel Hands plummets to his death **Mervyn Peake, 1949**

Israel Hands

Once back on board, Jim finds the ship guarded by just two pirates, both of whom are drunk and brawling. Jim's old enemy, Israel Hands, is the victor. He spots the lad and immediately sets out to kill him.

Jim escapes up the main mast, with Israel in pursuit. At the crow's nest, Jim can go no further and turns to face his foe. Israel throws his knife at him and, hitting him in the arm, pins him to the mast. Then the pistol Silver had given Jim goes off. It shoots Hands between the eyes and he crashes to his death. Jim then cuts the anchor line and, letting the Hispaniola drift across the bay, takes down the Jolly Roger and replaces it with the Union Jack. With the ship safe, he goes back to the stockade to meet up with his companions. Instead he ends up with Silver and his cutthroats.

Silver rescues Jim by pretending to take him hostage and then, under a flag of truce, gets Dr Livesey to tend his wound. The pirates disapprove and try to depose him as their leader. Silver outwits them, even after they have given him the Black Spot. Long John cunningly keeps a foot in both camps by pretending to keep Jim hostage, whilst siding with the doctor.

At the entrance to the **Bathurst Basin**, *and alongside one of Bristol's last remaining ancient slipways, the Trust would like to erect a ship's mast showing* **Israel Hands** *either chasing Jim up the mast with a knife in his mouth, or plummeting to his death. In* **The Basin**, *before the construction of the* **Floating Harbour** *two hundred years ago, was known as* **Trin Mills Pond** *and was where the* **Malago** *stream, coming from* **the Dundry** *slopes via* **Novers Hill**, *entered a still tidal river* **Avon**. *It was used by the Corporation for duck shoots and other entertainments.*

Treasure Island **Mervyn Peake, 1949**

G *A Survivor (Abraham Gray)*

Silver is still arguing with the crew about Jim. He accuses Merry, who wants to kill the lad, of being "brisk for business". Silver then takes Jim to one side and tells him that he's "as smart as paint". He produces the treasure map and then stands down as their leader. The pirates rush off to find the treasure.

Pointing the way on the macabre treasure trail are Flint's dead crew's corpses. The pirates are further "spooked" when they hear a ghostly voice (actually Ben Gunn) crying out the name of a former shipmate - "Darby McGraw".

They find an old sea chest but, after digging around, realise that the treasure is long gone. They then turn on their former leader and in the resulting fight Silver kills George Merry. He and Jim are then rescued by Livesey, Trelawney and their party - together with Ben Gunn. The castaway reveals that he has hidden the treasure in his cave and after rescuing the Squire's party takes them there as well.

You'll have to read Treasure Island for yourself if you want to know the ending...

*Mervyn Peake's excellent picture shows the survivors of the adventure taking the Treasure away to the **Hispaniola** in bread bags. **Abraham Gray** was one of the crew that Long John Silver tried to turn pirate. He escaped his clutches by the skin of his teeth.*

*On **Merchants Landing** (see page 31), perhaps guiding people from **Redcliffe Wharf** to the new **Museum of Bristol** on **Wapping Wharf**, the Trust would like to put a statue of an ordinary seaman carrying a load along the quayside - it could even be the treasure from Ben Gunn's cave. Even if you aren't on the trail it's a scene reminiscent of Bristol's maritime past.*

Achievements of the Trust

A Long John Silver sculpture was conceived way back in the nineties by Anne and Jerry Hicks, but the **Great Reading Adventure** spurred a number of individuals to take the matter forward and to set up *The Long John Silver Trust.* Since then the Trust has grown and created a number of activities and ideas to promote the objectives and to raise funds to purchase the *Bristol Treasure Island Trail* plaques and the *Long John Silver* sculpture.

The Painting
Well-known local maritime artist, **Frank Shipsides**, was commissioned to produce a painting showing what an imagined statue might look like, standing in front of the *'Hole in the Wall'* inn. The Trust started operations in September 2004 with a limited edition print run of the painting. Frank became our first Patron and sales of the painting led to the foundation of the Trust.

The Cruises
In 2006 the Trust organised, in conjunction with the Bristol Ferry Boat Company, river cruises for the pupils of Briarwood special needs School in Bristol, and the related charity PROPS, (Providing Opportunities and Support). The cruises, around the Floating Harbour, were to see the locations of the proposed sculptures, whilst members of the Trust performed a shortened version of Treasure Island for the pupils. The cruises have subsequently become a regular feature of the Trust's activities.

The audience bask in the sunshine after the performance.

64

The Voyage   It might not have been quite the High Seas, or even the blue Caribbean, but it had all the makings of a great day out. *The Long John Silver Trust* - a gang of charitable but home loving pirates – would accompany their patron Councillor Royston Griffey, Bristol's Lord Mayor, on a *"perambulation"* of the river Avon, Steep Holm, Flat Holm and Denny Island. This Michaelmas *"Beating the Bounds"* – a ceremony which hadn't been carried out for over 100 years - was meant to establish Bristol's historic sea boundaries. The Lord Mayor whose personal mission this was, had sensibly arranged to travel on the *HMS Ledbury* a naval minesweeper. She would be accompanied by the replica ship *Matthew*, various small craft from the Cabot Cruising Club and a dozen or so LJST members on board a 85 foot sailing ketch, the *Tangaroa*. Also invited; and hoping for some great shots and a big story, were a photographer and reporter from ITV West.

The first inkling that things might not be going quite to plan was when Trust members, arriving in their pirate outfits at a chilly and desolate- looking docks long before dawn, discovered the Lord Mayor already there, decked out in his finery and tucking into breakfast. The *Matthew* had been delayed and he had already started his perambulation down the Avon the previous evening courtesy of the *Tangaroa* and her small crew. Things started looked up when the Lord Mayor, before moving onto the *Ledbury*, kindly made the proud LJST members honorary **Sea Bailiffs.** The new bailiffs responded with a donation from their precious stock of grog; **Wickwar Long John Silver beer.**

Come dawn, which was anything but rosy - fingered, the boats locked out into a murky Bristol Channel. The *Ledbury*, lightly built of fibreglass and capable of a mighty 25 knots, soon disappeared into the mists leaving the Trust's ketch chugging along at a mere five. *"Don't worry,"* said experienced skipper Rick Wakeham. *"We'll hang around here, have some breakfast, and catch up with her when she returns from Denny Island and Steep Holm. She's due back into Avonmouth at 1.30pm. There's some wind so we'll put on some sail."* It was just then, as a surfeit of quickly eaten sausages and hot coffee coincided with a slight channel swell, that the Trust's Secretary Mark, lost his sea legs and a couple of sausages to boot. A fellow pirate was soon on hand to swab down the decks - and a comfy cabin found below decks in which to spend a few hours!

But it wasn't long before a far more serious disaster occurred. The ITV West crew's vegetarian sausages, specially bought along for the trip, had vanished, scoffed either by the ship's canine (the only real *"Sea-dog"* on board!) or even, perish the thought, by a veggie piratical Secretary! Perhaps they were even then floating towards the Portishead shores, being attacked by a platoon of piratical piranhas! This was just the start of a series of seafaring misfortunes. Was this, a man timorously ventured, because there were women on board, including the skipper's wife Helen? There was also a baby, William; quickly re - named *"Billy Bones"* after one of the pirates in *Treasure Island.* Were they bad luck too? There might have been a bit of gurgling but at least no female whistling - a sure, way as the old salts used to say, of bringing on a storm.

After miraculously rendezvousing with the Lord Mayor's ship, the *Tangaroa* headed for land - only to find that the tide was ebbing strongly. Against a swirling, swollen current of some 6 knots it soon became obvious that the ketch was making little headway - in fact she soon started going backwards, down channel! Eagle-eyed pirates, with the help of a spyglass, were soon reporting seeing the same shoreline landmarks, such as the old Portishead Nautical School, time after time. *"Never mind"* said the skipper *"We'll have some lunch cooked in the galley and wait for the tide to turn – it'll only be a few hours. You can watch our 'Pirates of the Caribbean' DVD's below decks if you want."*

Still dogged by bad luck, yet further misery was in store. The Cap'n commandeered the last bottle of grog!

"The fair breeze blew, the fair foam flew, the furrow followed free
*We weren't the first to suffer thirst upon that **Severn Sea** "*

Cap'n Rick hogs the last bottle of grog, whilst the envious crew look on!

But by now the ITV West duo had seen enough of life at sea. With their camera damp and out of action – Helen's hair-dryer did no good – perhaps because it whistled – arrangements were made for them to be transferred and taken ashore in a nippy Bristol Port survey boat. But bad luck still dogged them. Unbelievably the vessel ran out of fuel and they had to be rescued by a member of the Lord Mayor's flotilla, an old lifeboat. They certainly won't be venturing out into the Channel again in a hurry!

You might be wondering whether the LJST members - not forgetting little *"Billy Bones"* and the *"Sea-dog"* - ever get back onto dry land. Well, yes they did, but not until the tide turned in the late afternoon. By then, with dusk creeping in over the water, the grog was gone and the ship's hardtack supplies were running dangerously low. Saying goodbye to the *Tangaroa* and her crew meant perilously climbing a 30 foot high rusting iron ladder outside the Avonmouth lock gates - a fitting ending, surely to a memorable 13 hours on the *Severn Sea.*

The Podcast
The Trust worked with Bristol's tourist promotional agency **Destination Bristol** to produce a downloadable Podcast, about *Treasure Island* and the Trail. This was brilliantly narrated by former East Enders star *Simon Cook*, now a city councillor.

Bristol Books and Publishers
The Trust became members of Bristol's own publishers group and, as a result, has been associated with a number of publications and events. In 2006 the *Bristol Treasure Island Trail* was listed as the first of a number of interesting walks, in *Redcliffe Press's '24 Family Walks'.* In 2006 and 2007 the Trust joined BBP on a stall at the Bristol Harbourfest and is now working *with Fiducia Press* on a seminal book about pirates and piracy out of Bristol.

The Grog
In 2006 the Trust, in conjunction with *Wickwar Brewery,* launched its Long John Silver draught beer, to the slogan **'Hop till you Drop!'** The beer, with *'just a little extra hop'* to it, has been a tremendous success, with a proportion of the proceeds going to the Trust. More recently the beer has been produced in bottled form and is going faster than rum!

The Talks
The Trust has mounted a wide range of talks about its activities with local Rotary Clubs, Womens' Institutes, Youth organisations, Probus and other groups. Other events are planned with a view to raising the funds for the Treasure Island Trail and for the permanent sculptures.

The Wicker Sculpture
In 2007, to obtain greater publicity for the project, the Trust commissioned a wicker sculpture of **Long John Silver**. One-and-a-half times lifesize, the sculpture, by **Stephen Froome** of *'Wicked Willow'* in Devon, was delivered in February 2008 and has been exhibited at a wide range of events during the year He was unveiled for the first time for World Book Day in March 2008 at Waterstones Bristol Galleries shop by Lord Mayor of Bristol, Councillor Royston Griffey J.P.

Sebastian Peake, son of **Mervyn Peake,** whose interest in *Treasure Island* is described on page 6,was kind enough to become a Patron of the *Long John Silver Trust* soon after it was founded. In April 2008 Sebastian took part in Bristol's prestigious **Festival of Ideas City Museum Talk**, to the backdrop of our wicker sculpture which was on display nearby **in Borders Bookshop.**

Wicker Long John Silver launches World Book Day at Bristol Waterstones with the Lord Mayor and pupils from Hannah More Primary School.

In July 2008 the Bristol Hippodrome mounted a performance of Treasure Island by the Birmingham Stage Company and the event was launched by the Trust in conjunction with some of the PROPS children, with the wicker sculpture mounted on top of the theatre portico and illuminated by pyrotechnics.

Long John Graces the portico of Bristol's Hippodrome Theatre

Pieces of Eight

Bibliography

Albury, Paul. *'The Story of The Bahamas'* Macmillan Education Ltd 1975

Betty, J.H. *'Bristol Observed'* Redcliffe Press 1986

Brown, Harold G. *'Bristol, England'* Rankin Bros. Ltd. 1946

Cairney, John. *'The Quest for Robert Louis Stevenson'* Luath Press 2004

Craton, Michael. *'A History of the Bahamas'* (3rd Edition) San Salvador Press 1986

Dampier, William. *'A New Voyage Round the World'* London 1697

Defoe, Daniel. *'Robinson Crusoe'* London 1719

Earle, Peter. *'The Pirate Wars'* Methuen 2003

Greenacre, Francis. *'Maritime Artists of Bristol'* Redcliffe Press 1982

Hutton, Stanley. *'Bristol and its Famous Associations'* J.W. Arrowsmith 1907

Johnson, Captain. *'General History of Ye Pyrates'* London 1724

Jones, Donald. *'Captain Woodes Rogers' Voyage Round the World'* Bristol Branch of the Historic Association 1992

Manwaring, G.E. *'Woodes Rogers - Privateer and Governor'* Cassell and Co. Ltd 1928

Marley, David F. *'Pirates: Adventurers of the High Seas'* Arms and Armour Press 1995

McLynn, Frank. *'Robert Louis Stevenson'* Hutchinson 1993

Nicholls, J.F. and Taylor, John. *'Bristol Past and Present Vols II and III'* J.W.Arrowsmith 1882

Norris, Gerald. *'West Country Pirates and Buccaneers'* Dovecote Press 1990

Novak, Maximillian E. *'Daniel Defoe - Master of Fictions'* Oxford University Press 2001

Preston, Diana and Michael. *'A Pirate of Exquisite Mind'* Doubleday 2004

Rogers, Woodes. *'A Cruising Voyage Round the World'* London 1712

Souhami, Diana. *'Selkirk's Island'* Weidenfeld & Nicholson 2001

Stevenson, Robert Louis. *'Treasure Island'* Cassell & Co. Ltd. 1883

Stevenson, Robert Louis. *'Treasure Island'* Illustrated by Lyle
Justis Arden Book Co. 1930
Stevenson, Robert Louis. *'Treasure Island'* Illustrated by Mervyn
Peake Eyre & Spotiswoode 1949
Swift, Jonathon. *'Gullivers Travels'* London 1726

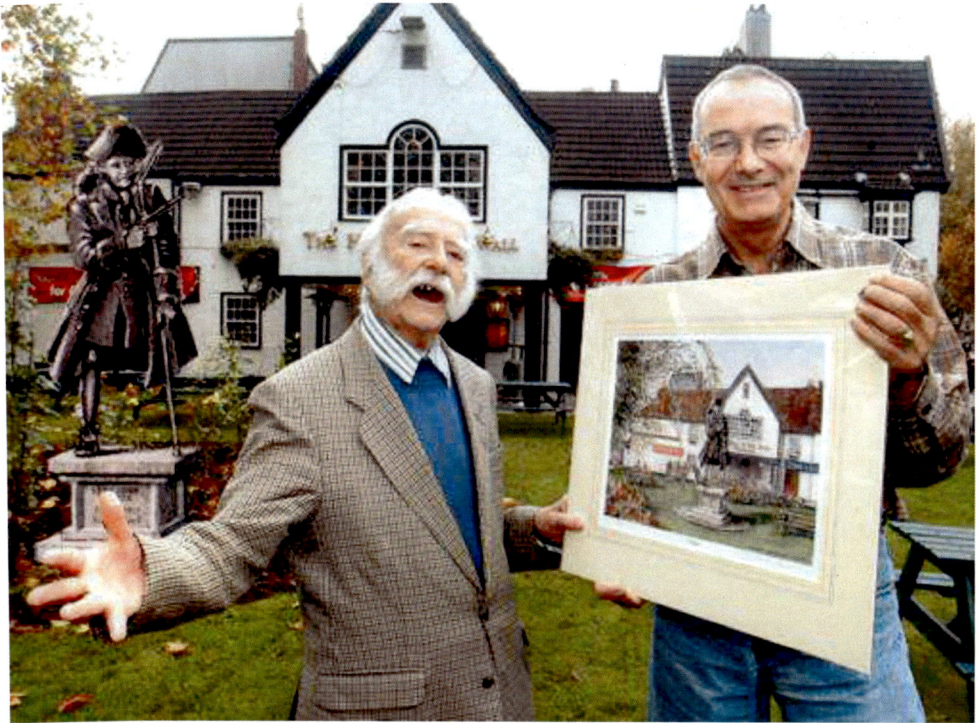

**The late Frank Shipsides, first Patron of the Long John Silver
Trust, handing over the first signed print of his painting
'Tribute' (1 of 70).**

**This shows Frank's impression of how a sculpture would look
in front of the *'Hole in the Wall'* pub.**

**Somehow, Long John himself has managed to get into the
action!**

Try a drop of Long John Silver Beer, available as draught from selected pubs in and around Bristol, or, more widely, as the very popular bottled beer.

Hop till you drop!

The Long John Silver Trust works closely with PROPS, the charity which specialises in sixth form students with severe learning difficulties, supporting inclusive projects.

http://www.props4ward.org